THE OFFICIAL Sunderlandafc ANNUAL 2011

This book belongs to

Age

Favourite player

Prediction of Sunderland's final position this season

Prediction of Barclays Premier League winners this season

Prediction of FA Cup winners this season

Prediction of Carling Cup winners this season

Prediction of teams to be relegated from the Barclays Premier League this season:

18th

19th

20th

Written by
Rob and Barbara Mason

A TWOCAN PUBLICATION

Published by Twocan under licence from Sunderland AFC.

ISBN 978-0-9559299-6-0

PICTURE CREDITS

Getty Images, North News, Twocan and Rob Mason.

£6.99

REAL

THE OFFICIAL Sunderlandafc ANNUAL 2011

CONTENTS

Sunderland
...2010-11 SQUAD

BACK ROW - LEFT TO RIGHT: Craig Russell (Masseur), Robbie Weir, Marcos Angeleri, Jordan Henderson, Anton Ferdinand, Simon Mignolet, Craig Gordon, Trevor Carson, Michael Turner, David Meyler, Paulo Da Silva, David Healy, Bill Wilson (Masseur)

MIDDLE ROW - LEFT TO RIGHT: David Binningsley (Senior Physio), Mike Clegg (Strength and Conditioning Coach), Jack Colback, John Mensah, Andy Reid, Fraizer Campbell, Darren Bent, Asamoah Gyan, Danny Welbeck, Kieran Richardson, Phil Bardsley, Keith Bertschin (Reserve Team Coach), Dave Galley (Senior Physio), Mark Boddy (Video Analyst)

FRONT ROW - LEFT TO RIGHT: Dr Glen Rae, Will Royall (Fitness Coach), Ahmed Elmohamady, Nedum Onuoha, Bolo Zenden, Eric Black (Assistant Manager), Steve Bruce (Manager), Lee Cattermole, Steed Malbranque, Cristian Riveros, Titus Bramble, Nigel Spink (Goalkeeping Coach), John Cooke (Kitman)

Darren made his debuts for Charlton and Spurs at the same ground ...the Stadium of Light ...and scored twice for Charlton
Dar
Totten
scorer
year
He scored his first ever goal in November 2001 for Ipswich ...against Newcastle!
Darren played for England at youth and U21 level as well as the full England team
He was once in an England U21 squad for a game at the Stadium of Light

as
s top
s last
spur

Darren Bent

SAFC's £10m Super Signing

Darren's middle name is Ashley

Darren began his career with Ipswich and then played for Charlton and Spurs before signing for Sunderland

Last season no player from outside the league's top seven clubs scored more than 10 goals - apart from Darren who scored 24!

He was born in Wandsworth in London on February 6th 1984

In 2005-2006 no English player scored more Premier League goals than Darren who scored 18 for Charlton

Wayne Rooney was the only English player to score more Barclays Premier League goals than Darren last season and Rooney is the only English player to score more times in the Premier League than Darren over the last five years

JOHN MENSAH

FACT FILE:

COUNTRY: Ghana
POSITION: Defender **SQUAD NO:** 5

WHERE WAS HE BORN?

John was born in a place called Obuasi which is in Ghana in West Africa. It is a hot country, just north of the Equator and has a lot of flat land and low hills.

WHAT IS HIS COUNTRY FAMOUS FOR?

The name Ghana means 'warrior king.' Ghana became independent from Great Britain in 1957 but English is still the official language with most people speaking one of the many local languages as well. Ghana is famous for gold as well as for producing cocoa and wood.

Has he played for his country?

Yes he played for them at the world cup finals in South Africa where he was their captain.

MARCOS ANGELERI

FACT FILE:

COUNTRY: Argentina
POSITION: Full back **SQUAD NO:** 12

WHERE WAS HE BORN?

Marcos was born in the capital of Argentina, Buenos Aires. It is one of the most famous and beautiful cities of South America and indeed the world. Argentina is a long country that stretches almost two and a half thousand miles down the east side of South America. In the north of the country it can be hot and humid but they get a lot of snow in the south.

WHAT IS HIS COUNTRY FAMOUS FOR?

Argentina is famous for the dance the tango, for raising cattle and for a person called Eva Peron who was the wife of a former president. There is a very famous stage show and film about her called 'Evita'. Ask your mam to sing you the song, 'Don't Cry for me Argentina'!

Has he played for his country?

Yes, before he signed for Sunderland, Marcos had played for his country three times.

PAULO DA SILVA

WHERE WAS HE BORN?

Paulo comes from Asuncion which is the capital of Paraguay in South America.

WHAT IS HIS COUNTRY FAMOUS FOR?

Paraguay has no border with the sea which means it is what is called 'land-locked' - completely surrounded by other countries. Brazil, Argentina and Bolivia are the three nations that border Paraguay. A lot of Paraguay's business is to do with farming.

Has he played for his country?

Yes Paulo is a regular player for Paraguay. He played for them at the world cup finals in South Africa and sometimes captains them.

FACT FILE:

COUNTRY: Paraguay
POSITION: Defender **SQUAD NO:** 14

Where I'm from

Sunderland AFC have several players from around the world

CRISTIAN RIVEROS

COUNTRY: Paraguay
POSITION: Midfield **SQUAD NO:** 16

WHERE WAS HE BORN?

Cristian comes from a place called Juan Augusto Saldivar. It is also sometimes known as Posta Leiva and is near the capital of Paraguay which is a city called Asuncion.

WHAT IS HIS COUNTRY FAMOUS FOR?

As well as football, Paraguay is famous for producing things for export from farming. It is a big country with not many people. From June to September the weather is mild in what is the dry season but for the rest of the year it is a hot country with a lot of rain.

Has he played for his country?

Yes he plays regularly for Paraguay and scored for them at the World Cup finals in South Africa.

ASAMOAH GYAN

WHERE WAS HE BORN?

Accra, which is the capital of Ghana in West Africa and is on the coast.

WHAT IS HIS COUNTRY FAMOUS FOR?

The coast Accra is on is called The Gold Coast. Ghana has produced a lot of gold. The country also has diamonds as well as cocoa and wood.

Has he played for his country?

If Ghana produces gold, Gyan produces goals. When he played his first game for Ghana as a Sunderland player in September it was the 47th time Asamoah had played for his country and up until then he'd scored 23 goals. Three of these goals were in the 2010 FIFA World Cup and at the 2006 World Cup he scored the quickest goal in the tournament.

COUNTRY: Ghana
POSITION: Striker **SQUAD NO:** 33

AHMED ELMOHAMADY

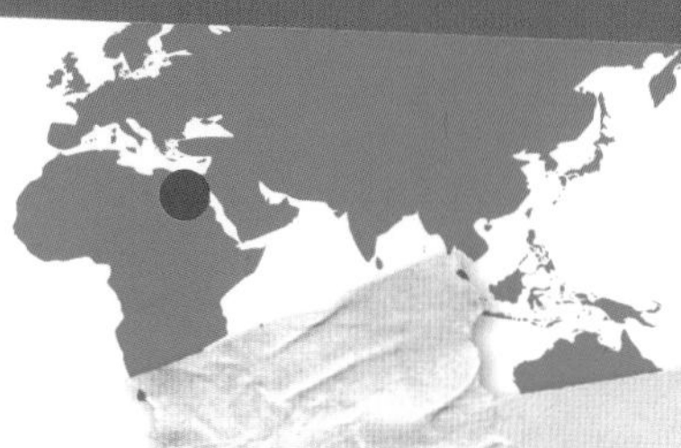

WHERE WAS HE BORN?

Elmohamady was born in a place called El-Mahalla El-Kubra which is in Egypt. Egypt is a hot country with much of it getting very little rain.

WHAT IS HIS COUNTRY FAMOUS FOR?

Egypt of course is famous as one of the world's great ancient civilisations. Think of the pyramids, camels, Tutankhamun and the Sphinx!

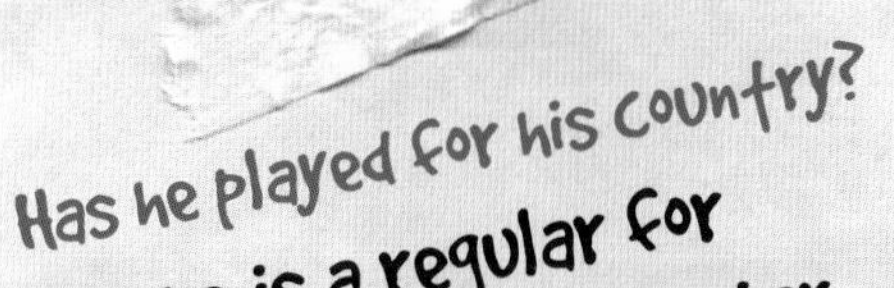

Has he played for his country?

Yes he is a regular for Egypt and is a superstar in his own country.

COUNTRY: Egypt
POSITION: Midfield **SQUAD NO:** 27

Colour the Crest ...and show your True Colours!

ASAMOAH
GYAN
tombola

Steve played 737 league games in his career...

309 of them were for Manchester United

Steve Bruce
...AS A PLAYER

- **His last game was against Sunderland**
- Scored an incredible 81 goals - he was a defender
- **Steve scored a lot of his goals from penalties and was famous for scoring powerful headers**
- As a young player he was rejected by several clubs - including Sunderland and Newcastle
- **As a boy he played in midfield**
- He became a centre back at his first club Gillingham and debuted in 1979
- **Steve spent six years playing for Gillingham, played over 200 times for them and is in their 'Hall of Fame'**
- In 1984 Steve was sold to Norwich ...and scored an own goal in the first minute of his debut against Liverpool!
- **He made up for it by scoring the winner against local rivals Ipswich in the League Cup semi-final the same season**
- In the final at Wembley Steve won a winner's medal against ...Sunderland

- **He's in Norwich's 'Hall of Fame'**
- Man United bought Bruce in 1987
- **He won the Premier League with them three times**
- He won the FA Cup three times
- **He became the first English player of the twentieth century to captain a team to the 'double' of league title and FA Cup in the same season in 1993-94**

- He won the League Cup with Manchester United as well as Norwich
- **Steve had been a ball boy at the 1974 League Cup final when Wolves beat Manchester City when he was 14**
- He won the European Cup Winners' Cup and European Supercup with Man Utd
- **He played for England in the 1980 European U18 championship**
- He once captained England 'B' against the full international side of Malta

Steve Bruce

...AS A MANAGER

- First became a manager with Sheffield United in 1998
- **His next job was at Huddersfield**
- Steve managed Wigan twice, once in 2001 and then again from 2007 to 2009
- **After his first spell as Wigan manager, Steve managed Crystal Palace**
- From 2001 to 2007 Steve managed Birmingham City winning promotion twice, once on penalties against Norwich where he'd once been a favourite
- **He became Sunderland manager in 2009**
- He signed class players like Darren Bent, John Mensah, Lee Cattermole and Cristian Riveros for Sunderland
- **Steve's assistant manager is Eric Black who is a Scottish international**
- In his first season he guided Sunderland to their highest position for nine years
- **Sunderland's victory over Manchester City in August was the 200th of Steve's career as a manager**

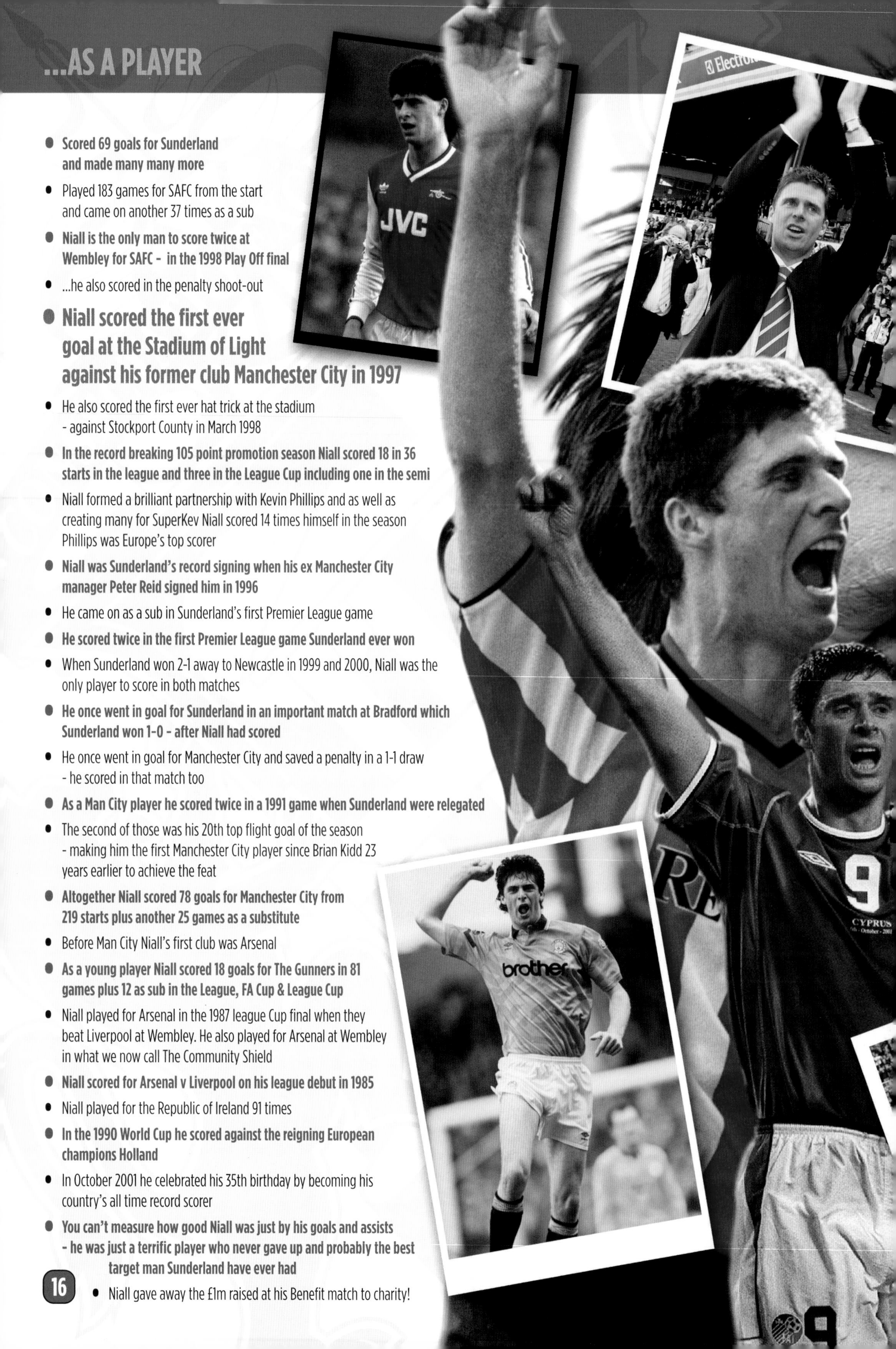

...AS A PLAYER

- **Scored 69 goals for Sunderland and made many many more**
- Played 183 games for SAFC from the start and came on another 37 times as a sub
- **Niall is the only man to score twice at Wembley for SAFC - in the 1998 Play Off final**
- ...he also scored in the penalty shoot-out
- **Niall scored the first ever goal at the Stadium of Light against his former club Manchester City in 1997**
- He also scored the first ever hat trick at the stadium - against Stockport County in March 1998
- **In the record breaking 105 point promotion season Niall scored 18 in 36 starts in the league and three in the League Cup including one in the semi**
- Niall formed a brilliant partnership with Kevin Phillips and as well as creating many for SuperKev Niall scored 14 times himself in the season Phillips was Europe's top scorer
- **Niall was Sunderland's record signing when his ex Manchester City manager Peter Reid signed him in 1996**
- He came on as a sub in Sunderland's first Premier League game
- **He scored twice in the first Premier League game Sunderland ever won**
- When Sunderland won 2-1 away to Newcastle in 1999 and 2000, Niall was the only player to score in both matches
- **He once went in goal for Sunderland in an important match at Bradford which Sunderland won 1-0 - after Niall had scored**
- He once went in goal for Manchester City and saved a penalty in a 1-1 draw - he scored in that match too
- **As a Man City player he scored twice in a 1991 game when Sunderland were relegated**
- The second of those was his 20th top flight goal of the season - making him the first Manchester City player since Brian Kidd 23 years earlier to achieve the feat
- **Altogether Niall scored 78 goals for Manchester City from 219 starts plus another 25 games as a substitute**
- Before Man City Niall's first club was Arsenal
- **As a young player Niall scored 18 goals for The Gunners in 81 games plus 12 as sub in the League, FA Cup & League Cup**
- Niall played for Arsenal in the 1987 league Cup final when they beat Liverpool at Wembley. He also played for Arsenal at Wembley in what we now call The Community Shield
- **Niall scored for Arsenal v Liverpool on his league debut in 1985**
- Niall played for the Republic of Ireland 91 times
- **In the 1990 World Cup he scored against the reigning European champions Holland**
- In October 2001 he celebrated his 35th birthday by becoming his country's all time record scorer
- **You can't measure how good Niall was just by his goals and assists - he was just a terrific player who never gave up and probably the best target man Sunderland have ever had**
- Niall gave away the £1m raised at his Benefit match to charity!

Niall Quinn ...THE LEGEND

...AS MANAGER

- **When Niall took over as Sunderland chairman he decided to start his first season as manager until he could get the manager he wanted**
- Niall had five competitive games as manager
- **Infamously Sunderland lost the first four**
- Niall won his final match as manager against West Brom so he went out on a high!

...AS CHAIRMAN

- **Sad to see the club he had learned to love struggling Niall organised a group of businessmen to take over in 2006**
- When Niall took over the club, SAFC had just been relegated with a record low number of points and it took a magnificent effort to get the club heading in the right direction again
- **Niall persuaded Roy Keane to become a manager for the first time**
- Sunderland won the Championship in Quinn's first season as chairman and Keane's first as manager
- **Sunderland did well in their first season back in the Premier League but before the second season was half over Niall needed a new manager after Roy Keane left**
- Niall asked Ricky Sbragia to keep Sunderland in the Premier League and he achieved that before stepping down
- **In the summer of 2009 Steve Bruce became SAFC manager**
- Since deciding to become chairman Niall has overseen two changes of ownership of the club as he has worked hard behind the scenes to help Sunderland
- **Niall has been a major influence on Sunderland's bid to be a 2018 World Cup venue**
- Niall has helped Sunderland to three times break the club transfer record with the signings of Craig Gordon, Darren Bent and Asamoah Gyan
- **No matter how busy he is, Niall has still succeeded in having time for every supporter and a massive hero to all of them**

The Squad ...2010-2011

CRAIG GORDON

POSITION: Goalkeeper
DATE OF BIRTH: December 31st 1982
BIRTHPLACE: Edinburgh
SIGNED FROM: Hearts
OTHER CLUBS: Cowdenbeath on loan

Craig has won more caps for Scotland than any other player while on Sunderland's books.

SCOTLAND INTERNATIONAL

SQUAD NUMBER 1

KIERAN RICHARDSON

POSITION: Left back
DATE OF BIRTH: October 21st 1984
BIRTHPLACE: Greenwich (London)
SIGNED FROM: Manchester United
OTHER CLUBS: WBA on loan

Kieran won a Barclays Premier League medal in 2007 and the Carling Cup a year earlier. In 2003 he scored in the final as Man Utd won the FA Youth Cup.

SQUAD NUMBER 3

PHIL BARDSLEY

POSITION: Right back
DATE OF BIRTH: June 28th 1985
BIRTHPLACE: Salford
SIGNED FROM: Manchester United
OTHER CLUBS: Burnley, Rangers, Aston Villa, Sheffield Utd - all on loan.

Phil made his full Barclays Premier League debut for Manchester United against Sunderland at the Stadium of Light.

SQUAD NUMBER 2

MICHAEL TURNER

SQUAD NUMBER 4

POSITION: Centre back **DATE OF BIRTH:** November 9th 1983
BIRTHPLACE: Lewisham (London) **SIGNED FROM:** Hull City
OTHER CLUBS: Charlton Athletic, Leyton Orient (loan), Brentford

In every season from 2003-04 to 2008-09 Michael won at least one club Player of the Year award.

JOHN MENSAH

SQUAD NUMBER 5

POSITION: Centre back
DATE OF BIRTH: November 29th 1982 **BIRTHPLACE:** Obuasi, Ghana
SIGNED FROM: On loan from Olympique Lyon
OTHER CLUBS: MBC Accra, Bologna, Bellinoza (loan), Genoa (loan), Chievo Verona, Modena (loan), Cremonese, Rennes

In November 2006 John was named as the best defender in French football.

GHANA INTERNATIONAL

LEE CATTERMOLE

SQUAD NUMBER 6

ENGLAND U21 INTERNATIONAL

POSITION: Central midfield
DATE OF BIRTH: March 23rd 1988 **BIRTHPLACE:** Stockton
SIGNED FROM: Wigan Athletic **OTHER CLUBS:** Middlesbrough

Lee played for Sunderland as a boy at the old 'Charlie Hurley Centre' before he ever joined Boro.

BOUDEWIJN ZENDEN

POSITION: Central or left midfield

DATE OF BIRTH: August 15 1976 **BIRTHPLACE:** Maastricht, Netherlands

SIGNED FROM: Unattached but last club was Marseille

OTHER CLUBS: PSV Eindhoven, Barcelona, Chelsea, Boro, Liverpool

Bolo has played in the Champions League final and the semi finals of the World Cup and the European Championships.

NETHERLANDS INTERNATIONAL

FRAIZER CAMPBELL

POSITION: Striker or winger

DATE OF BIRTH: September 13th 1987

BIRTHPLACE: Huddersfield

SIGNED FROM: Manchester United

OTHER CLUBS: Antwerp, Hull City, Spurs, all on loan

Fraizer made his Premier league debut for Manchester United in a derby against Manchester City but suffered a bad injury playing for Sunderland against the same opposition this season.

ENGLAND U21 INTERNATIONAL

SQUAD NUMBER 9

FRANCE U21 INTERNATIONAL

SQUAD NUMBER 8

STEED MALBRANQUE

POSITION: Midfield

DATE OF BIRTH: January 6th 1980 **BIRTHPLACE:** Mouscron, Belgium

SIGNED FROM: Tottenham Hotspur **OTHER CLUBS::** Lyon, Fulham

Steed made his home debut for Fulham against SAFC in 2001 and played at Sunderland for Fulham on a day the match was abandoned because of snow in 2006.

JORDAN HENDERSON

POSITION: Central or right midfield
DATE OF BIRTH: June 17th 1990
BIRTHPLACE: Sunderland
SIGNED FROM: Trainee
OTHER CLUBS: Coventry (loan)

Jordan was a ball boy at the Stadium of Light when England played Turkey in 2003.

SQUAD NUMBER
10

ENGLAND U21 INTERNATIONAL

DARREN BENT

POSITION: Striker
DATE OF BIRTH: February 6th 1984
BIRTHPLACE: Wandsworth (London)
SIGNED FROM: Tottenham Hotspur
OTHER CLUBS: Ipswich, Charlton

Darren's debuts for Charlton and Tottenham Hotspur were both against Sunderland at the Stadium of Light.

SQUAD NUMBER
11

MARCOS ANGELERI

POSITION: Right back **DATE OF BIRTH:** April 7th 1983
BIRTHPLACE: La Plata, Buenos Aires Province (Argentina)
SIGNED FROM: Estudiantes (Argentina)
OTHER CLUBS: None

Marcos was named in the top 10 players in South America in 2008.

SQUAD NUMBER
12

ARGENTINA INTERNATIONAL

PAULO DA SILVA

POSITION: Centre back or full back

DATE OF BIRTH: February 1st 1980

BIRTHPLACE: Ascuncion (Paraguay)

SIGNED FROM: Toluca (Mexico)

OTHER CLUBS: Atlandida SC, Cerro Porteno, Olimpia, Perugia, Lanus, Venezia, Cosenza (loan), Libertad (loan)

Paulo won the league in Paraguay with Libertad in 2002 and the league in Mexico with Toluca in 05 and 08.

SQUAD NUMBER 14

PARAGUAY INTERNATIONAL

CRISTIAN RIVEROS

POSITION: Centre midfield

DATE OF BIRTH: October 16th 1982

BIRTHPLACE: J. A. Saldivar (Paraguay)

SIGNED FROM: Cruz Azul (Mexico)

OTHER CLUBS: Tacuary, San Lorenzo, Libertad

Cristian scored against Slovakia in the 2010 World Cup when he helped his country reach the quarter finals.

SQUAD NUMBER 16

NEDUM ONUOHA

POSITION: Right back or centre back

DATE OF BIRTH: November 12th 1986

BIRTHPLACE: Warri (Nigeria)

SIGNED FROM: On loan from Manchester City

OTHER CLUBS: None

Nedum has eight grade A GCSEs, two Bs and three A grades at A level.

SQUAD NUMBER 15

ENGLAND U21 INTERNATIONAL

SQUAD NUMBER 18

DAVID MEYLER

REPUBLIC OF IRELAND U21 INTERNATIONAL

POSITION: Centre midfield

DATE OF BIRTH: May 25th 1989 **BIRTHPLACE:** Cork

SIGNED FROM: Cork City **OTHER CLUBS:** None

David will miss the first half of the 2010-11 season after being injured against Manchester United at the end of last season. He had just been called up or the full Republic of Ireland squad for the first time when he got injured.

DANNY WELBECK

ENGLAND U21 INTERNATIONAL

POSITION: Striker

DATE OF BIRTH: November 26th 1990

BIRTHPLACE: Manchester

SIGNED FROM: On loan from Manchester Utd

OTHER CLUBS: Preston North End (loan)

Danny debuted for Manchester United's U18 side against Sunderland in April 2006.

SQUAD NUMBER 17

SQUAD NUMBER 19

ENGLAND U21 INTERNATIONAL

TITUS BRAMBLE

POSITION: Centre back

DATE OF BIRTH: July 31st 1981

BIRTHPLACE: Ipswich **SIGNED FROM:** Wigan Athletic

OTHER CLUBS:: Ipswich Town, Colchester Utd (loan) Newcastle Utd

Titus played for Steve Bruce at Wigan and won the player of the year award with the Latics.

ANDY REID

POSITION: Centre or left midfield **DATE OF BIRTH:** July 29th 1982

BIRTHPLACE: Dublin **SIGNED FROM:** Charlton Athletic

OTHER CLUBS: Tottenham Hotspur

Andy scored his final goal for Nottingham Forest against Sunderland.

SIMON MIGNOLET

POSITION: Goalkeeper

DATE OF BIRTH: August 6th 1988

BIRTHPLACE: Saint-Trond (Belgium)

SIGNED FROM: Sint Truiden (Belgium)

OTHER CLUBS: None

Goalie Simon once took a penalty in a Belgian league game, saw it saved but scored the rebound.

TREVOR CARSON

POSITION: Goalkeeper

DATE OF BIRTH: March 5th 1988 **BIRTHPLACE:** Downpatrick

SIGNED FROM: Trainee **OTHER CLUBS:** Chesterfield, loan

INTERNATIONAL: Northern Ireland U21. Also been in full squads.

Trevor occasionally played as an emergency striker when in the youth team.

27

EGYPT INTERNATIONAL

AHMED ELMOHAMADY

POSITION: Right midfield or right back
DATE OF BIRTH: September 9th 1987
BIRTHPLACE: El-Mahalla El-Kubra (Egypt)
SIGNED FROM: ENPPI on season long loan
OTHER CLUBS: Ghazl El-Mehalla

Elmohamady won the African Cup of Nations with Egypt in 2010.

ENGLAND U21 INTERNATIONAL

ENGLAND U20 INTERNATIONAL

SQUAD NUMBER

25

JACK COLBACK

POSITION: Centre or left midfield
DATE OF BIRTH: October 24th 1989
BIRTHPLACE: Newcastle
SIGNED FROM: Trainee
OTHER CLUBS: Ipswich, loan

Won the Players' Player of the Year ' award when on loan to Ipswich last season.

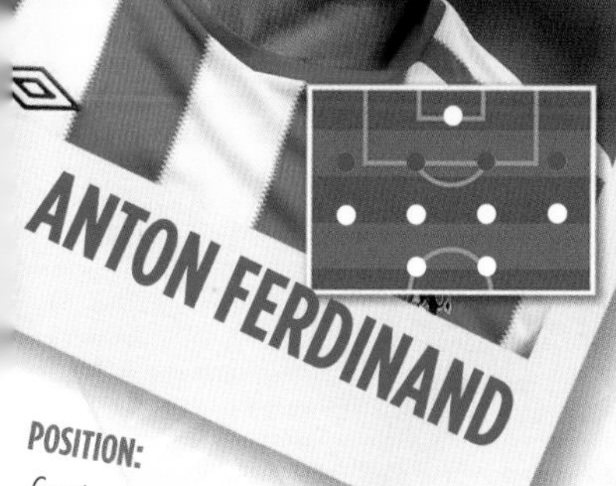

ANTON FERDINAND

POSITION: Centre back or full back
DATE OF BIRTH: Feb 18th 1985 **BIRTHPLACE:** Peckham
SIGNED FROM: West Ham Utd **OTHER CLUBS:** None
INTERNATIONAL: England U21

Anton of course is the brother of England captain Rio and has 17 England U21 caps of his own.

SQUAD NUMBER

33

ASAMOAH GYAN

POSITION: Striker
DATE OF BIRTH: November 22nd 1985
BIRTHPLACE: Accra (Ghana)
SIGNED FROM: Rennes
OTHER CLUBS: Liberty Professionals, Udinese, Modena (loan)

In the 2010 World Cup quarter final against Uruguay, Gyan missed a penalty in the last minute and then had the mental strength to step up and take the first one in the shoot out a few minutes later - and scored.

GHANA INTERNATIONAL

SPOT THE Difference

Can you spot the eight differences between these pictures?

ANSWERS ON PAGE 62.

Identity ...CRISIS!

Stars in their eyes...

Can you identify these four Sunderland Stars from their eyes alone?

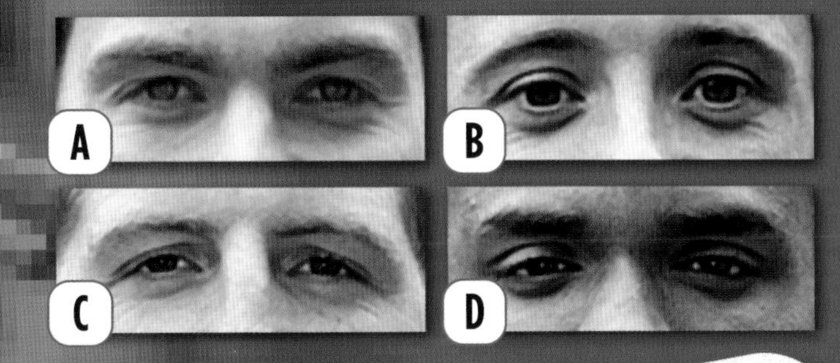

Who am I? Mega pixels

TAKE 2

Two Black Cats are mixed up in each of these head shots!

Can you identify them all?

ANSWERS ON PAGE 62.

Have you got a brother? Which of you is the best player?

How would you both like to play for SAFC?

Brotherly ...LOVE

It's happened before but not very often. In fact there have only ever been five league or cup games when Sunderland have had two brothers on the pitch at the same time.

Earlier this season when Sunderland beat Manchester City, the visitors had two brothers playing for them in Kolo and Yaya Toure while when England won the World Cup in 1966 the famous Charlton brothers of Bobby and Jackie were both in the side.

There have only ever been five sets of brothers who have both played for Sunderland and not all of them have played in the same team at the same time. Marco Gabbiadini for instance was a great striker in the late 1980s and early 1990s but the only time his brother Ricardo played for the first team he came on as a substitute for his brother. Imagine that: you are playing for Sunderland when the signal goes for you to come off ...and be replaced by your brother!

1973 AND ALL THAT

When Sunderland won the FA Cup in 1973 the top scorer that season was Billy Hughes. His elder brother John had been a big star for Celtic and was signed by Sunderland during the cup winning season. Unlike the Gabbiadini brothers the Hughes brothers did play together - but just for a few minutes. John was injured very early on in his first game and never played again. Billy played 335 times for Sunderland, scoring 81 goals. Both played for Scotland but not in the same match.

PEACOCK BROTHERS

Andrew and William Peacock played in the very early days of the club. It was so long ago Sunderland hadn't even joined the Football League. The Peacock brothers became the first to play for Sunderland in a competitive game when they played in the FA Cup against a team called Elswick Rangers as long ago as 1888. Sunderland won 5-3 with Andrew scoring twice. This was the only competitive game William played for Sunderland although both brothers played a lot of friendly games which is what Sunderland mainly played at this time.

There are another nine players who have played for SAFC first team who have had brothers who have been on the books but only playing reserve or junior football for the club. One of these was Jonjo Dickman who played once for Sunderland at Manchester City in 2003. His brother Elliott was a promising young player whose career was ended by injury. Elliott went into coaching and is now assistant academy manager at Sunderland.

JOHN HUGHES

BILLY HUGHES

Marco scored 87 goals in 185 games for the Black Cats.

MARCO AND RICARDO

BROTHERS WHO HAVE PLAYED FOR SUNDERLAND	
FIRST TEAM PLAYER	**BROTHER**
Ben Alnwick	Jak played U18
Clive Bircham	Bernard played during WW2
Frank Cresswell	
Warney Cresswell	
William Cringan	James had unsuccessful trial in 1920
Jonjo Dickman	Elliot - played for reserves
William Fullarton	David - played for reserves
Marco Gabbiadini	
Ricardo Gabbiadini	
Mick Henderson	Ken - played for reserves
Billy Hogg	John - played for reserves
Billy Hughes	
John Hughes	
Bobby Marshall	John - played for reserves
Andrew Peacock	
William Peacock	
Ephraim Rhodes	Ernest - played for reserves
Anthony Smith	
Dan Smith	

THE GABBIADINI BROTHERS almost played together in an away match at Leeds in 1989 only for Marco to be the man substituted when Ricardo came on for what was his only first team game for Sunderland.

THE SMITH BROTHERS

Dan Smith played five games for Sunderland in the 2005-06 season. Like his brother Anthony he was a left back. Anthony appeared 25 times between 1988 and 1995.

CRESSWELL BROTHERS

Warney and Frank Cresswell played in the 1920s. Warney was the most famous of the pair and played for England. For Sunderland he played nearly 200 times and later won the league while playing for Everton. While Warney was a right back, his brother Frank was an attacking left sided player who played for England as a schoolboy international. Although he only played 13 times he did score for Sunderland - something his brother never achieved.

Their first of only three games together for Sunderland was away to Huddersfield in September 1926. Less than five months later Warney was sold to Everton

BOUDEWIJN ZENDEN

WHERE WAS HE BORN?

Bolo was born in Maastricht in the Netherlands. Maastricht is famous because in 1992 when Bolo was 15, Maastricht was the place in Europe where the leaders of the European countries met to form what is known as 'The Maastricht Treaty which led to the creation of the Euro.

WHAT IS HIS COUNTRY FAMOUS FOR?

The Netherlands is famous for its flowers, especially tulips. It is also well known for having a relaxed lifestyle and has major European cities in Amsterdam and Rotterdam. It is also famous for its football of course. The Netherlands have been in three World Cup finals including last summer's in South Africa. You often hear people calling the Netherlands Holland but in fact North Holland and South Holland are just part of the Netherlands.

Has he played for his country?

He certainly has although he is now retired from international football. Zenden represented his country 54 times scoring seven goals. He played in a World Cup semi final against Brazil in 1998 and two years later against Italy in a European Championship semi final.

FACT FILE:

COUNTRY: Netherlands
POSITION: Midfield
SQUAD NUMBER: 7

STEED MALBRANQUE

WHERE WAS HE BORN?

Steed was born in a place called Mouscron in Belgium but he considers himself French as he explains: "My parents were working in Belgium when I was born so that is how I was born there. My mother is Italian and my dad is French so that is how I moved to France when I was five years old."

HAS HE PLAYED FOR HIS COUNTRY?

Steed has played for France at U21 level including the European U21 final in 2002. He captained them at the U18 age group and was called up for the full squad in February 2004 but has never won a full cap.

What is his country famous for?

France is famous for so many things including champagne, wine, cheese, French bread and of course the tourist sites of the capital city Paris such as the Arc de Triumphed and the Eiffel Tower. France is a beautiful country of contrasts with scenic mountains such as Mont Blanc, stunning coastline and charming villages.

FACT FILE:

COUNTRY: France
POSITION : Midfield
SQUAD NUMBER: 8

Where I'm from

Sunderland have three players from European countries other than those in Great Britain and the Republic of Ireland.

SIMON MIGNOLET

WHERE WAS HE BORN?

Simon was born in a place called Saint-Trond in Belgium. Belgium is a small, flat country between France and the Netherlands.

The three main languages spoken are Flemish, French and German.

HAS HE PLAYED FOR HIS COUNTRY?

It seems only a matter of time until he plays for the Belgium team. He is the U21 goalkeeper and kept six clean sheets in his first eight games for them.

COUNTRY: Belgium
POSITION: Goalkeeper
SQUAD NUMBER: 22

What is his country famous for?

The headquarters of the European Community is based in the city of Brussels. Belgium has many very attractive cities such as Bruges and Antwerp and is famous for its beer, chocolate and waffles. Have you seen the great cartoon series 'Tinting'? That was produced by a Belgian artist called Georges Remit who wrote under the name of 'Herve'.

DID YOU KNOW...

Sunderland is where glass was first used in Britain? That was at St. Peter's Church and it's one of the reasons Sunderland is now the home of the National Glass Centre.

Sunderland was once the biggest shipbuilding port in the world?

A ship twice as big as the Titanic was once built at Sunderland? It was called The Naess Crusader and was 110,000 tons.

Another ship built at Sunderland was called The Torrens. Have you seen the pub in Sunderland named after it? This ship was written about by the novelist Joseph Conrad and for 15 years it was the fastest ship on the planet.

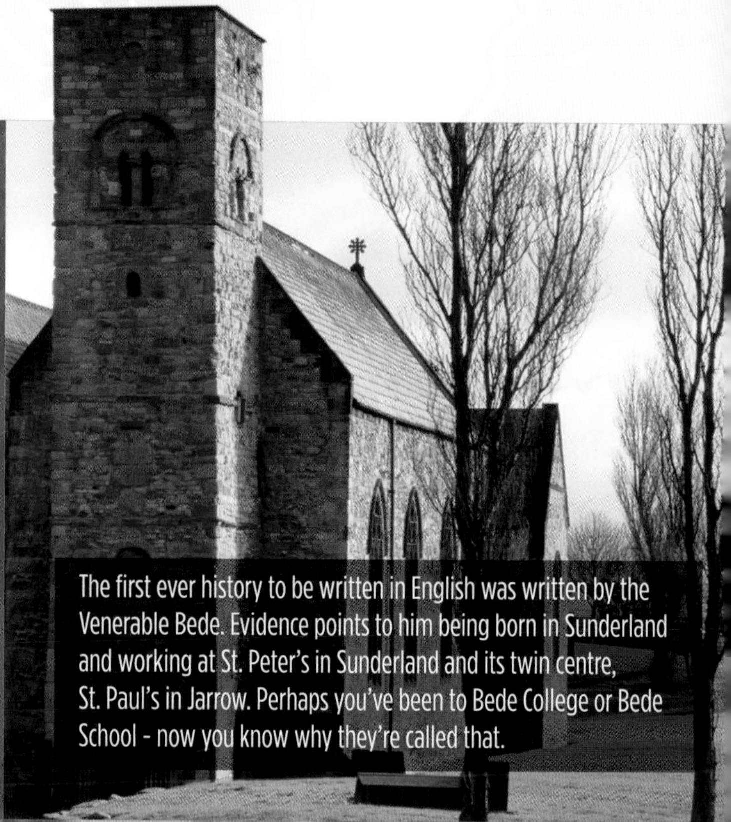

The first ever history to be written in English was written by the Venerable Bede. Evidence points to him being born in Sunderland and working at St. Peter's in Sunderland and its twin centre, St. Paul's in Jarrow. Perhaps you've been to Bede College or Bede School - now you know why they're called that.

Take a look at the walrus from Alice in Wonderland in Mowbray Park in Sunderland. Lewis Carroll the famous writer used to come to Whitburn for his holidays. The 'Alice' of Alice in Wonderland is believed to be Alice Pleasance Liddell, the daughter of Henry Liddell, Dean of Christ Church, Oxford where Lewis Carroll was a professor. Lewis Carrol visited Alice's relations who lived in Whitburn Hall while he was staying with his own cousins who also lived in Whitburn. Ever wondered what the word Wonderland in 'Alice in Wonderland' sounds like?

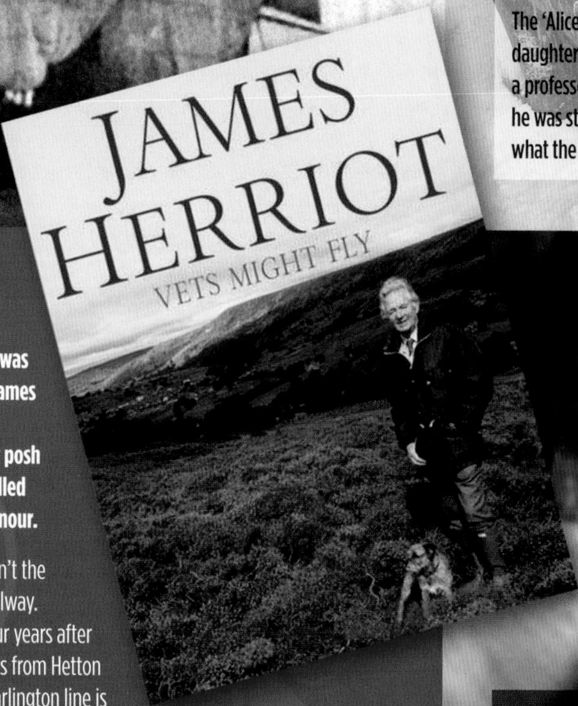

JAMES HERRIOT
VETS MIGHT FLY

James Herriot who wrote the famous books about vets that became a very popular TV series was from Sunderland. Really called James Alfred Wight he was a massive Sunderland supporter and a very posh part of the Stadium of Light is called The James Herriot Suite in his honour.

The world's first ever railway wasn't the famous Stockton to Darlington railway. That opened in 1836 and came four years after the world's first railway which was from Hetton to Sunderland. The Stockton to Darlington line is famous because it was the world's first passenger railway. The one from Hetton to Sunderland was to transport coal but it was the first.

Joseph Swan who invented the electric light bulb independently of Thomas Edison, was born in Sunderland.

POLICE PUBLIC CALL BOX

Do you like Dr Who? How about the Tardis? Did you know the first ever 'Tardis style' police box was made in Sunderland?

The Sunderland international airshow is the biggest free airshow in Europe.

Where you are from

On pages 10 & 11 and 30 & 31 we've found out a little bit about where Sunderland's overseas players are from. Where are you from and what is your home town like?

If you are from Sunderland like Jordan Henderson you've got a lot to be proud of.

LS Lowry, the famous artist used to come to Seaburn for his holidays. He painted a lot of pictures in Sunderland and there's one in the Board room at the Stadium of Light.

Washington which is part of Sunderland is where the first president of the USA came from. He was called George Washington and the original Washington is the only place in Europe to have signed a Friendship Agreement with Washington DC in the USA where Barack Obama now serves in the White House. The red and white strips on the flag of the USA originate from George Washington's coat of arms.

Charles Alcock - the man who came up with the idea of the FA Cup - the oldest football trophy in the entire world - came from Sunderland.

The record attendance for a football match in the North East of England was at Sunderland: 75,118 for an FA Cup tie with Derby County.

Can you finish this picture of Black Cat Steed Malbranque and colour it in?

STEED

MALBRANQUE

www.oceanicogolf.com
128
O'CONNOR
FUSION

...it's Golf!
SAFC STYLE

For many footballers the idea of an afternoon on the golf course after training seems like heaven.

Being footballers of course they take the competition very seriously and are always really keen to come out on top so there's plenty of rivalry but the main thing is everyone has a great time.

JAMES ARMSTRONG

POSITION: Centre midfield

DATE OF BIRTH: May 10th 1993

BIRTHPLACE: Sunderland

Only eight players have ever played more games for Sunderland than James' dad Gordon

LEWIS KING

POSITION: Goalkeeper

DATE OF BIRTH: May 8th 1993

BIRTHPLACE: Derby

Played for Derby before moving to Sunderland

JOHN EGAN

POSITION: Centre back

DATE OF BIRTH: October 20th 1992

BIRTHPLACE: Cork

John has played for the Republic of Ireland at U16 and U17 level

LOUIS LAING

POSITION: Centre back, can play midfield

DATE OF BIRTH: March 3rd 1993

BIRTHPLACE: Newcastle

Louis has played for England at U16 and U17 level

BRETT ELLIOTT

POSITION: Midfield

DATE OF BIRTH: May 30th 1993

BIRTHPLACE: South Shields

Big powerful left sided player

MICHAEL LAMB

POSITION: Centre back

DATE OF BIRTH: March 18th 1993

BIRTHPLACE: Sunderland

No nonsense defender who played regularly last season

ALEJANDRO RODRIGUEZ GORRIN

POSITION: Centre midfield

DATE OF BIRTH: August 1st 1993

BIRTHPLACE: Tenerife

Talented skilful player

LIAM MARRS

POSITION: Right back

DATE OF BIRTH: November 26th 1992

BIRTHPLACE: Cramlington

Liam attracted interest from Newcastle United before joining Sunderland

ANDREW HARRISON

POSITION: Centre midfield/right back

DATE OF BIRTH: September 4th 1992

BIRTHPLACE: Sunderland

Attracted interest from Leeds and Hartlepool before joining SAFC

JORDAN WATSON

POSITION: Left back or left midfield

DATE OF BIRTH: April 7th 1993

BIRTHPLACE: Cyprus

Jordan has represented Northern Ireland at U15, U16 and U17 level

Sunderland's Academy is a very successful place that develops young players

During 2010 Jordan Henderson, Martyn Waghorn, Jack Colback, George McCartney, Michael Liddle and Ryan Noble have all played for the first team having at one time been youth team players at Sunderland and goalkeeper Trevor Carson is another Academy player who has regularly been on the bench with Adam Reed another player to make the bench but not quite the team so far.

Academy manager Ged McNamee together with assistants Elliott Dickman and Kevin Ball; Sunderland's former captain, work very hard over many years with their coaching staff to bring on young players sometimes from as young as eight years old. Every year there are a group of young players who have done very well to make it as far as the Under 18 team and who are hoping to progress into the first team. Keep your eyes out for these players. Who knows in a year or two they might be thrilling you at the Stadium of Light.

JAMES BRACE

POSITION: Centre midfield

DATE OF BIRTH: November 17th 1993

BIRTHPLACE: Hartlepool

Began coming to the Sunderland Academy as an eight year old

JORDAN LAVENDER

POSITION: Centre back

DATE OF BIRTH: October 8th 1993

BIRTHPLACE: Colchester

Went to Framwellgate Moor School in Durham and started at SAFC's Academy when he was 10

ANTHONY CALLAGHAN

POSITION: Left back

DATE OF BIRTH: May 2nd 1994

BIRTHPLACE: Sunderland

Anthony has played for England at U16 level

ADAM MITCHELL

POSITION: Centre forward

DATE OF BIRTH: October 18th 1993

BIRTHPLACE: Middleton in Teasdale

Played regularly last season while still at school

JOEL DIXON

POSITION: Goalkeeper

DATE OF BIRTH: December 9th 1993

BIRTHPLACE: Middlesbrough

Has been coming to the Academy of Light since he was 14

CONNOR OLIVER

POSITION: Defender

DATE OF BIRTH: January 17th 1994

BIRTHPLACE: Newcastle

Attracted interest from Leicester City, Doncaster Rovers and St. Mirren before joining Sunderland

JORDAN LAIDLER

POSITION: Striker

DATE OF BIRTH: October 13th 1993

BIRTHPLACE: North Shields

With Sunderland since he was 11 and broke into the U18 team last season when still at school

JORDAN PICKFORD

POSITION: Goalkeeper

DATE OF BIRTH: March 7th 1994

BIRTHPLACE: Washington

Jordan has represented England at U16 level

BLAIR ADAMS

POSITION: Left back
DATE OF BIRTH: September 8th 1991
BIRTHPLACE: South Shields

Strong defender who offers a real threat when he gets forward

BEN WILSON

POSITION: Goalkeeper
DATE OF BIRTH: August 9th 1992
BIRTHPLACE: Shotley Bridge

Cancelled his own 18th birthday party last summer to be on the bench for the first team in a pre-season friendly

LIAM BAGNALL

POSITION: Right back
DATE OF BIRTH: May 17th 1992
BIRTHPLACE: Newry

Capped at U15, U16, U17 and U19 level by Northern Ireland

NATHAN WILSON

POSITION: Midfield
DATE OF BIRTH: March 2nd 1992
BIRTHPLACE: Darlington

Determined player who was a regular at U18 level last season

MATTHEW FLETCHER

POSITION: Striker
DATE OF BIRTH: May 12th 1992
BIRTHPLACE: Sydney, Australia

Australian U20 international who got 16 goals at U18 level last season

JORDAN COOK

POSITION: Striker or midfield
DATE OF BIRTH: March 20th 1990
BIRTHPLACE: Easington Lane

Gained league experience with Darlington last season before injury curtailed his campaign

CRAIG LYNCH

POSITION: Midfield
DATE OF BIRTH: March 25th 1992
BIRTHPLACE: Durham

Creative player with a good footballing brain but has been restricted by injuries

MICHAEL KAY

POSITION: Right back or centre back
DATE OF BIRTH: September 19th 1989
BIRTHPLACE: Shotley Bridge

Gained England honours at U17 and U18 and played for first team in the FA Cup two seasons ago

RYAN NOBLE

POSITION: Striker
DATE OF BIRTH: November 6th 1991
BIRTHPLACE: Sunderland

Made first team debut in FA Cup last season and went on loan to Watford without getting a game

MICHAEL LIDDLE

POSITION: Left back
DATE OF BIRTH: Christmas Day 1989
BIRTHPLACE: London

Republic of Ireland international who has been on loan to Carlisle, played for SAFC in the FA Cup last season and started this season on loan to Leyton Orient.

Young PROFESSIONALS

Most of these players have progressed through the Sunderland academy system and are now playing for the Sunderland's reserves under the guidance of former players Keith Bertschin and Stephen Clemence.

The next step for them is to gain league experience out on loan and try to push on towards first team level at Sunderland.

NATHAN LUSCOMBE

POSITION: Left midfield

DATE OF BIRTH: November 6th 1989

BIRTHPLACE: New Hartley, Gateshead

Played for the first team in the FA Cup two seasons ago. Likes to run at defenders

DAN MADDEN

POSITION: Centre back

DATE OF BIRTH: September 10th 1990

BIRTHPLACE: Durham

Strong defender who can also play a holding midfield role

OUMARE TOUNKARA

POSITION: Striker

DATE OF BIRTH: May 25th 1990

BIRTHPLACE: Paris

Formerly with Sedan in France. On a season long loan to Oldham

LIAM NOBLE

POSITION: Centre midfield

DATE OF BIRTH: May 8th 1991

BIRTHPLACE: Newcastle

On the bench for the first team at Chelsea last season. No relation to Ryan

JEAN-YVES M'VOTO

POSITION: Centre back

DATE OF BIRTH: September 6th 1988

BIRTHPLACE: Paris

Former Paris St Germain player. On loan to Southend last year and now on a season long loan to Oldham

ADAM REED

POSITION: Midfield

DATE OF BIRTH: May 8th 1991

BIRTHPLACE: Hartlepool

An unused sub at first team level several times last season

ROBBIE WEIR

POSITION: Midfield or right back

DATE OF BIRTH: December 12th 1988

BIRTHPLACE: Belfast

Capped at U17, U19, U20 and U21 level by Northern Ireland. Played for the first team in pre-season.

1 **You take your first ever kick of a ball when you are maybe two years old...**

and your nana says "That was good, you'll be a footballer one day!"

Ladder ...TO SUCCESS

2 When you are a bit older you have your first ever kick-about with your mates in the school yard.

3 **You go for a trial for your school team and a couple of days later you see your name on the notice board - you've been picked!**

4 You do well for your school team, play every game and people notice you. You do your best for the team not yourself.

5 **When you are seven your parents or guardians and you get asked if you would start coming to train at Sunderland AFC.**

6 You have to keep fit, eat healthily and go to bed early - every day. It's not easy and you have to really want to do be a footballer and be prepared to do the right things.

7 **You work hard every day to develop your skills like dribbling and controlling the ball.**

8 You stick in and regularly attend one of SAFC's development centres at Sacriston, Sunderland University (Sunderland) and Gateshead college as well as at the Academy of Light.

9 **When you reach the Under 9 age group you sign on to be an academy player.**

10 Once you are signed you can begin to play in official academy games.

11 **It's hard work but you do well enough to progress through the age groups.**

20 Have you made it yet?

You've just played a few games and want to keep playing regularly for another 10 years or more. You remember what Jordan Henderson said when he won the Young Player of the Year award for the second time last season and earned a five year contract:

"I've only been in the first team one season so I certainly don't think I've cracked it and can relax. I'd be daft to think that. Next year will be a big challenge for me to see if I can push on even more. I have the right people around me to keep my feet on the ground and I'm confident I can improve."

That is the kind of attitude that gets you to the top - and once you lose that attitude you start sliding down the ladder rather than climbing up it.

19 You get called up for the England Under 19 team as your ability has been noticed nationally.

18 You impress enough to earn a regular place in the team and even though you are playing against big, strong, talented players you are doing well.

17 You come back to Sunderland and start to play a few games for the first team, you even score your first goal and celebrate like mad – after all you've been working for ten years already to get this far.

16 You join another team in the Championship or League One for a spell on loan and you do well.

15 You stand out in the reserves and one day are named as a substitute for the first team in the Carling Cup.

14 You do well enough to get picked for the reserve team which means some of the players you are playing against will be much older than you and probably bigger and stronger than you.

13 You begin to play for the Under 18 team. You might even play your first game at The Stadium of Light in the FA Youth Cup.

12 When you leave school you get asked to do a two year Scholarship which means becoming a full time footballer for the first time and continuing with your studies.

Think you could do Steve Bruce's job?

1	Craig Gordon	GOALKEEPER
2	Phil Bardsley	DEFENDER
3	Kieran Richardson	DEFENDER
4	Michael Turner	DEFENDER
5	John Mensah	DEFENDER
6	Lee Cattermole	MIDFIELDER
7	Boudewijn Zenden	MIDFIELDER
8	Steed Malbranque	MIDFIELDER
9	Fraizer Campbell	STRIKER
10	Jordan Henderson	MIDFIELDER
11	Darren Bent	STRIKER
12	Marcos Angeleri	DEFENDER
14	Paulo Da Silva	DEFENDER
15	Nedum Onuoha	DEFENDER
16	Cristian Riveros	MIDFIELDER
17	Danny Welbeck	STRIKER
18	David Meyler	MIDFIELDER
19	Titus Bramble	DEFENDER
20	Andy Reid	MIDFIELDER
22	Simon Mignolet	GOALKEEPER
24	Trevor Carson	GOALKEEPER
25	Jack Colback	MIDFIELDER
27	Ahmed Elmohamady	MIDFIELDER
29	Anton Ferdinand	DEFENDER
33	Asamoah Gyan	STRIKER

What would you be like at building a team?

Who would you sign for Sunderland? Fancy buying Wayne Rooney up front? Would you be able to talk Manchester United into selling him? Could you convince Rooney to swap the red and white of Man Utd for the red and white of SAFC or might someone like Real Madrid or Barcelona also want him and spoil your plans? Even if you could get him to come to Sunderland could you afford him? Really? You're getting too much pocket money!!!

You are going to need a pair of dice for this game so find a couple in some of your board games (but don't forget to put them back).

If you don't have a dice don't be put off. Get six bits of paper all the same size, write a number from one to six on each of them and then squash them up and put them in a bag. All anyone has to do when it's their turn is close their eyes and pick a bit of paper out of the bag to see what number they have. Remember to squash the paper up and put it back in the bag each time... might be easier to go and get a dice though!

This is a game for two players. The idea is to build a better team than your friend. Here goes:

Each have a roll of both of the dice. Whoever gets the highest number in total gets to go first. If you get the same total when you add both dice together try again. Roll your first dice. The number you get tells you how many times you can roll your second dice, for instance if you get a three with your first dice it means you have to roll your second dice three times.

Roll your second dice the number of times you have to according to the number of your first dice. Add together the scores of your second dice.

Picking SIDES

For example if you roll your second dice three times and get a 4, 2 and 5 that comes to 11 so you could pick player number 11 which is Darren Bent. To get Craig Gordon you'd need to get a 1 with your first dice followed by another 1 with your second. For Asamoah Gyan who is number 33 you'd need a 6 with your first dice followed by a total score of 33 with the six rolls of your second dice, so 5 sixes and a three would do it or maybe three fives and three sixes.

If the number you roll doesn't match the name of a player then you don't get to pick a player that time and have to wait until your next turn. If your number gives you a player you don't want in your team then you don't have to pick him but you have to wait until it's your turn again to have another go.

As you take turns and pick players fill them in on your team sheet. Once a player is picked the other player in this game can't have them. For instance you both can't pick Darren Bent.

Put players in their proper positions, for instance Lee Cattermole should be a midfielder. Once you've filled a section in (eg midfield) you can swap players in that section if you get the chance of a player you think is better than the one you already have but you have to keep them in their proper positions. It's not much use putting Malbranque in goal for instance!

When one of you has all eleven players filled in the other player has one more turn to complete their team. They only get one extra turn and if they still need more than one player then that's just tough!

Now you have to decide who has picked the best team. Well if one of you doesn't have 11 players it's not likely to be you. If you can't decide you'll need a referee so you'll have to ask whoever takes you to the match who they think has picked the best side.

TRANSFERS...

If you roll two sixes in one go well obviously there isn't a number 66 to choose but two sixes allows you to sign someone. If you roll two sixes that earns you the chance to make a signing.

Once you've rolled two sixes you get an extra turn. Add the scores of the pair of dice together from your extra turn and then you can sign anyone you like from the following lists , so long as your opponent hasn't already signed them. You can't both have the same player in your team.

Score 10,11 or 12

PICK FROM: Joe Hart, Nemanja Vidic, Frank Lampard, Cesc Fabregas, Didier Drogba or Wayne Rooney.

Score 7, 8 or 9

PICK FROM: Mark Schwarzer, Jonny Evans, James Milner, Andrei Arshavin, Robin van Persie or Robbie Keane.

Score 4, 5 or 6

PICK FROM: Ben Foster, Ledley King, Dickson Etuhu, El-Hadji Diouf, Marlon Harewood or Steven Fletcher.

Score 2 or 3

PICK FROM: Anyone in the Championship.

THE HISTORY OF SAFC

IN 1958 SUNDERLAND ARE RELEGATED FOR THE FIRST TIME IN THE CLUB'S HISTORY - THEY HAD NEVER PLAYED ANYWHERE BUT IN THE TOP DIVISION.
WHERE IS DIVISION TWO DAD?
READ ALL ABOUT IT!
NEWS THEY'RE DOWN
PICK THAT ONE OUT YOUNG MAN!
BRIAN CLOUGH - A GREAT GOAL SCORER FOR SUNDERLAND AND LATER EUROPEAN CUP WINNING MANAGER AT NOTTINGHAM FOREST.
LED BY CHARLIE HURLEY - LATER VOTED AS SUNDERLAND'S PLAYER OF THE CENTURY, THE CLUB ARE PROMOTED BACK INTO THE TOP DIVISION IN 1964.
GOOD OLD CHARLIE HURLEY HE SHOULD BE OUR PLAYER OF THE CENTURY.
IN 1973 AND BACK IN THE OLD SECOND DIVISION, SUNDERLAND SHOCK SOCCER BY WINNING THE F.A. CUP AGAINST MIGHTY LEEDS...
GREAT SAVE MONTY!
HOW'D HE GET TO THAT?
... WITH JIM MONTGOMERY MAKING THE MOST FAMOUS SAVE EVER SEEN AT WEMBLEY AS IAN PORTERFIELD SCORES THE GOLDEN GOAL.
CHEER UP PETER REID.
SUNDERLAND CLINCH PROMOTION IN 1976 BY BEATING A BOLTON TEAM WHO INCLUDED A VERY YOUNG PETER REID!
IT'S THE END!!
1985 AND SUNDERLAND LOSE IN THE LEAGUE CUP FINAL 1-0 TO NORWICH, HAVING MISSED A PENALTY. TO MAKE MATTERS WORSE, THE CLUB IS RELEGATED AGAIN HAVING ALSO BEEN RELEGATED IN 1977 AND PROMOTED IN 1980! THEN THE UNTHINKABLE HAPPENS, ONCE MIGHTY SUNDERLAND DROP INTO DIVISION THREE.
MISSED IT!
A GOAL FOR MARCO, WE'RE IN THE PLAY-OFF FINAL!
IN 1988, MARCO GABBIADINI IS THE NEW HERO AS HIS GOALS FIRE SUNDERLAND TO IMMEDIATE PROMOTION. IN 1990 SUNDERLAND BEAT NEWCASTLE IN THE PLAY-OFFS AND ARE PROMOTED AFTER PLAY-OFF FINAL WINNERS SWINDON ARE FOUND GUILTY OF FINANCIAL IRREGULARITIES.
IN 1992 JOHN BYRNE SCORES IN EVERY ROUND OF THE F.A. CUP EXCEPT THE FINAL...
... AS LIVERPOOL BEAT SUNDERLAND 2-0!
PETER REID BECOMES MANAGER IN 1995 AND A YEAR LATER WINS THE FIRST DIVISION CHAMPIONSHIP. IN 1999 SUNDERLAND WIN THE CHAMPIONSHIP AGAIN AFTER AN UNLUCKY RELEGATION WITH A RECORD NUMBER OF POINTS AND A PLAY-OFF FINAL DEFEAT ON PENALTIES.
WE'RE UP TO STAY THIS TIME!
IN 1997 SUNDERLAND MOVE TO THE SPACE AGE STADIUM OF LIGHT, THE BIGGEST AND BEST NEW GROUND BUILT IN ENGLAND!
2000 AND SUPER KEVIN PHILLIPS WINS THE EUROPEAN GOLDEN BOOT FOR SCORING 30 GOALS IN THE PREMIERSHIP.
IN 2006 FORMER CENTRE FORWARD NIALL QUINN TOOK OVER AS CHAIRMAN AND NOW IN 2010 SUNDERLAND ARE IN THE BARCLAYS PREMIER LEAGUE WITH STAR PLAYERS LIKE DARREN BENT AND ASAMOAH GYAN.

The Stadium of Light doesn't just have football. For the last two years it has also staged the biggest concerts in the North East.

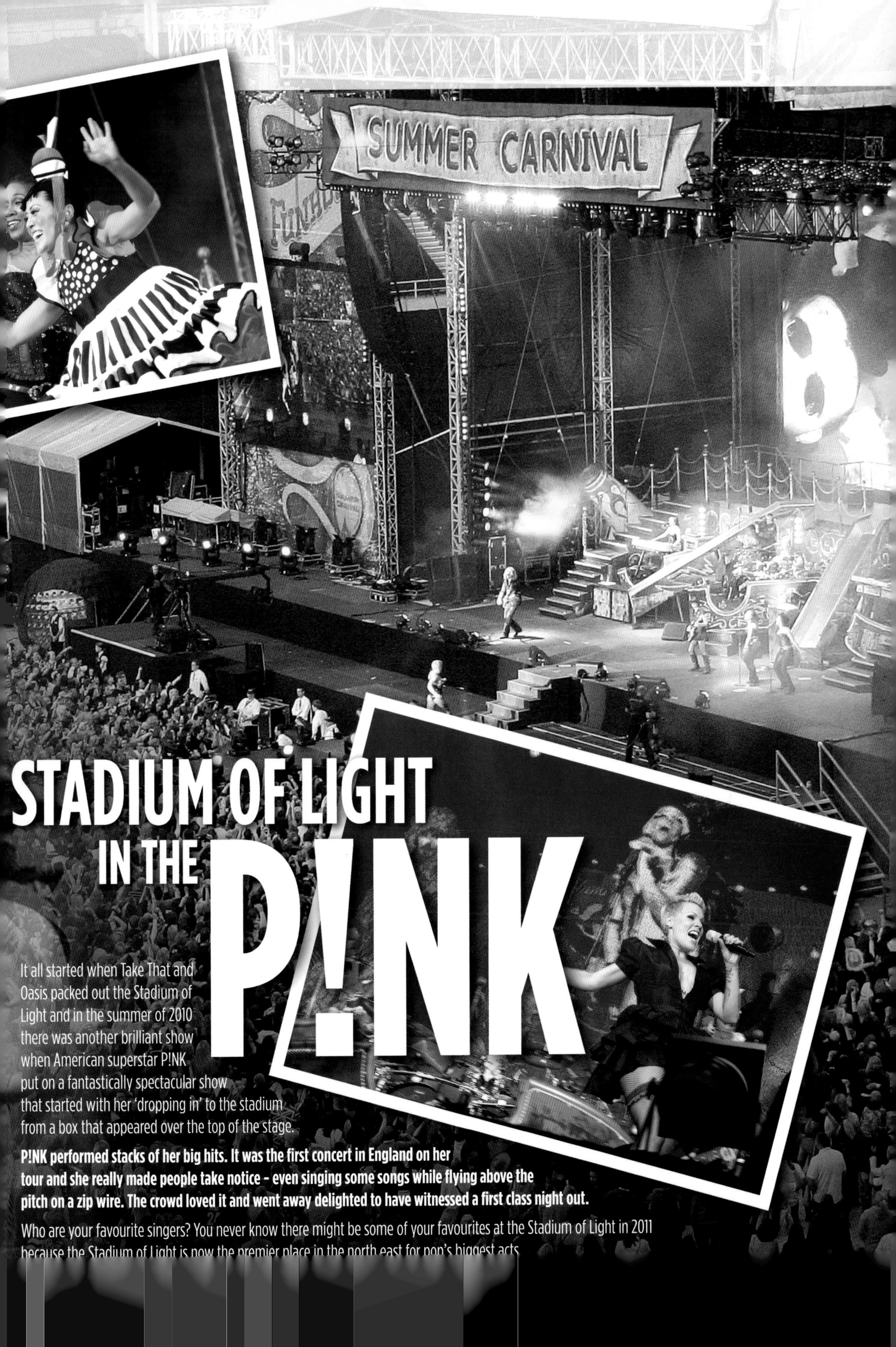

STADIUM OF LIGHT IN THE P!NK

It all started when Take That and Oasis packed out the Stadium of Light and in the summer of 2010 there was another brilliant show when American superstar P!NK put on a fantastically spectacular show that started with her 'dropping in' to the stadium from a box that appeared over the top of the stage.

P!NK performed stacks of her big hits. It was the first concert in England on her tour and she really made people take notice – even singing some songs while flying above the pitch on a zip wire. The crowd loved it and went away delighted to have witnessed a first class night out.

Who are your favourite singers? You never know there might be some of your favourites at the Stadium of Light in 2011 because the Stadium of Light is now the premier place in the north east for pop's biggest acts.

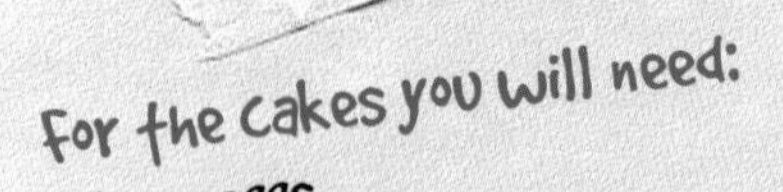

For the cakes you will need:

- 2 large eggs
- 1 teaspoon Vanilla essence
- 125 gm caster sugar
- 125 gm soft margarine
- 125 gm self raising flour
- A small pack of white ready to roll icing sugar
- A small pack of coloured icing sugar including red and black

You will also need:

- 12 paper cake cases
- A 12 hole bun baking tray
- Electric whisk if you have one or a wooden spoon
- Mixing bowl
- Rolling pin
- Small glass or cup
- Sharp knife

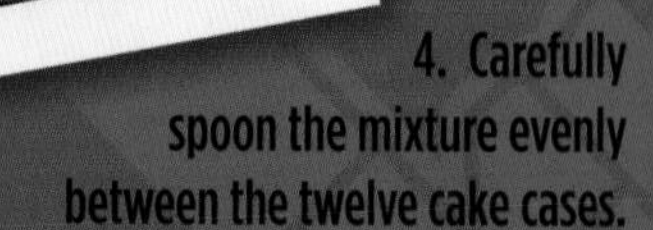

4. Carefully spoon the mixture evenly between the twelve cake cases.

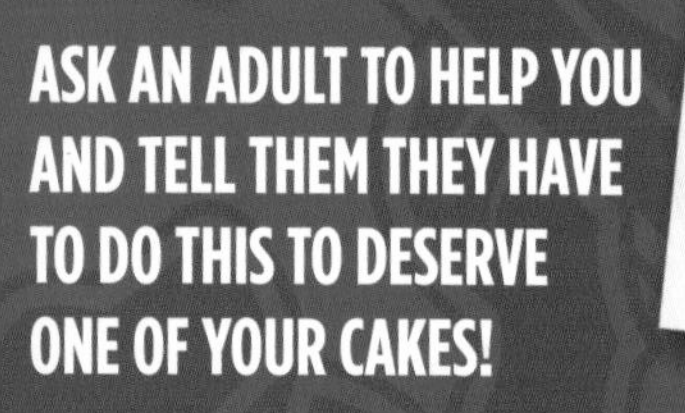

ASK AN ADULT TO HELP YOU AND TELL THEM THEY HAVE TO DO THIS TO DESERVE ONE OF YOUR CAKES!

1. Wash your paws!
2. **Pre-heat the oven to 180°C/350°F/Gas mark 4**
3. Place the eggs, vanilla essence, sugar, margarine and flour in a mixing bowl and beat together with an electric mixer until the mixture is smooth. This will take a few minutes. If you don't have a mixer you can use a wooden spoon but this will take longer and is a bit harder to do. (You may need to get an adult to help with this especially if you are using an electric mixer.)

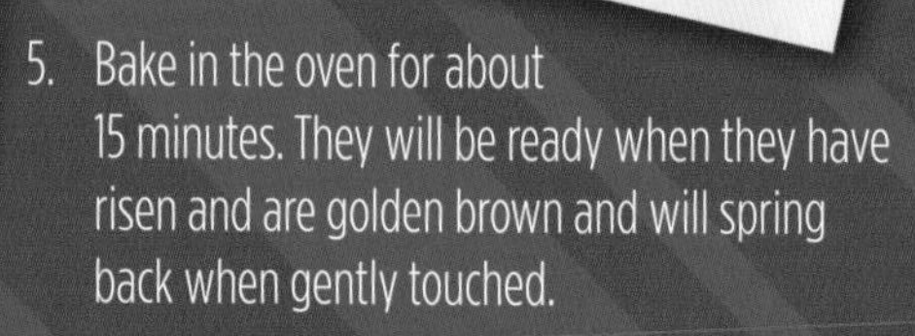

5. Bake in the oven for about 15 minutes. They will be ready when they have risen and are golden brown and will spring back when gently touched.
6. **Leave to cool for about 30 minutes before decorating.**

7. Roll out the white icing with the rolling pin until it is about 0.25cm thick.
8. **Use the top of a glass or cup as a template and cut out twelve circles using the sharp knife.**

Samson shows you how to make...

Easy Peasy ...CUP CAKES

9. Place one on top of each cupcake.

10. Use the coloured icing to decorate the top of the cakes.

Here are some ideas for you to try...

ARSENE WENGER

Top title teams
...CHAMPIONS OF ENGLAND

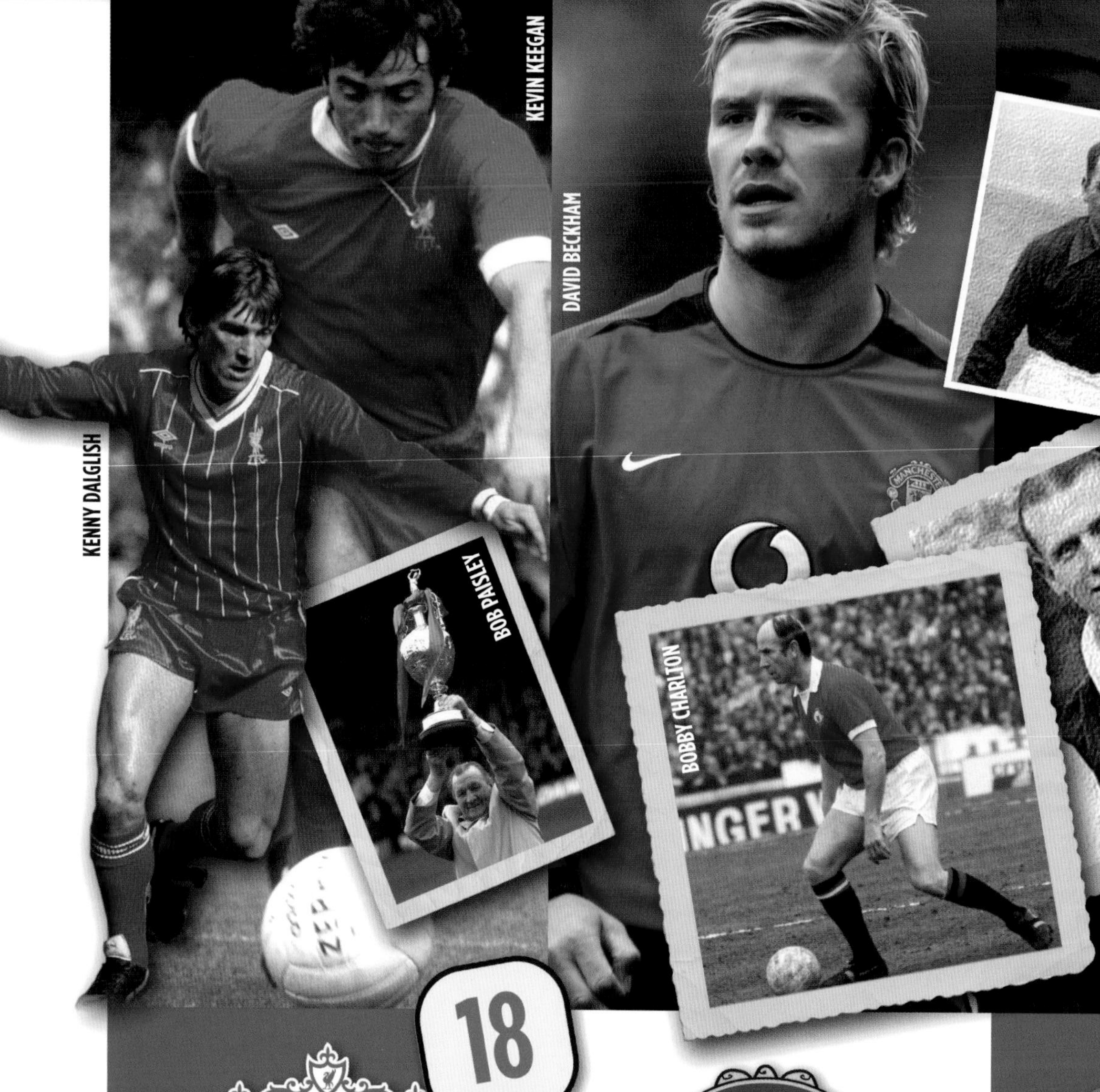

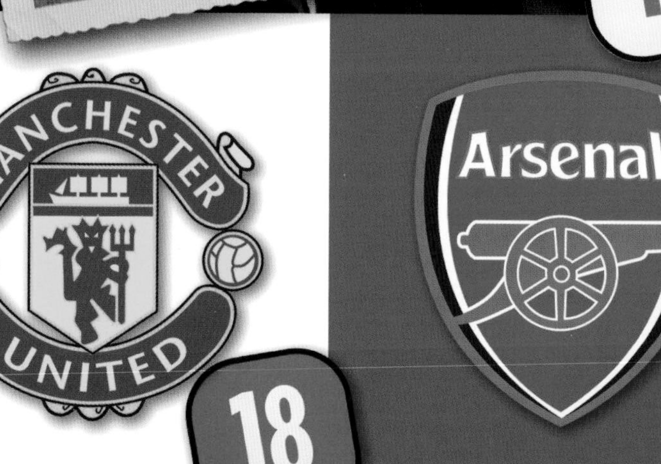

To be the champions of England is something extremely special. These days the clubs with the serious Champions League money tend to win the Barclays Premier League but even a team like Chelsea who have won the Premier League on three occasions have only been champions of England a total of four times. Since league football began way back in 1888, a total of 23 teams have been champions of England, many of them achieving this feat just the once. Only six teams have been champions in the top flight of English football more than four times and one of those is Sunderland.

Manchester United and Liverpool are out on their own as the most successful clubs although Liverpool have never won the Premier League.

For Sunderland to be one of the top six just shows why Sunderland have always been one of the biggest clubs in the land.

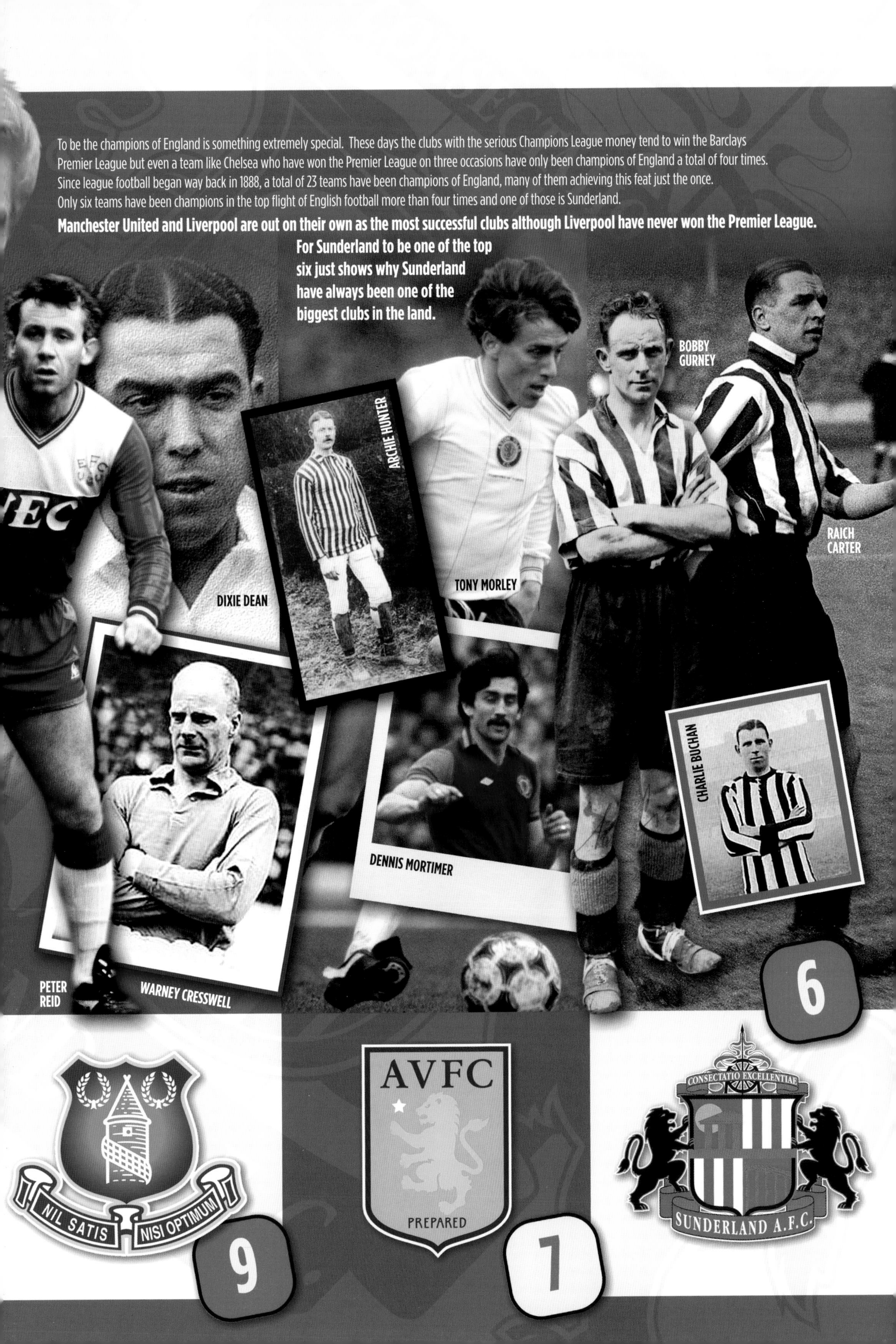

Who was Sunderland's top scorer last season?

1

Including cup goals did he score 20, 25 or 30 goals last season?

2

Which club did Steve Bruce play for when he won three Premier League titles?

3

Who became the most expensive goalkeeper in British football when he signed for Sunderland in 2007?

4

Who is the current player who used to play for Lyon, Fulham and Spurs?

5

Which four players have played for Sunderland this season after playing in the World Cup last summer?

6

Which countries did they play for?

7

Which current Sunderland player is an international for Egypt?

8

Which current Sunderland player scored twice on his debut for England?

9

Who has won Sunderland's Young Player of the Year award for the last two seasons?

10

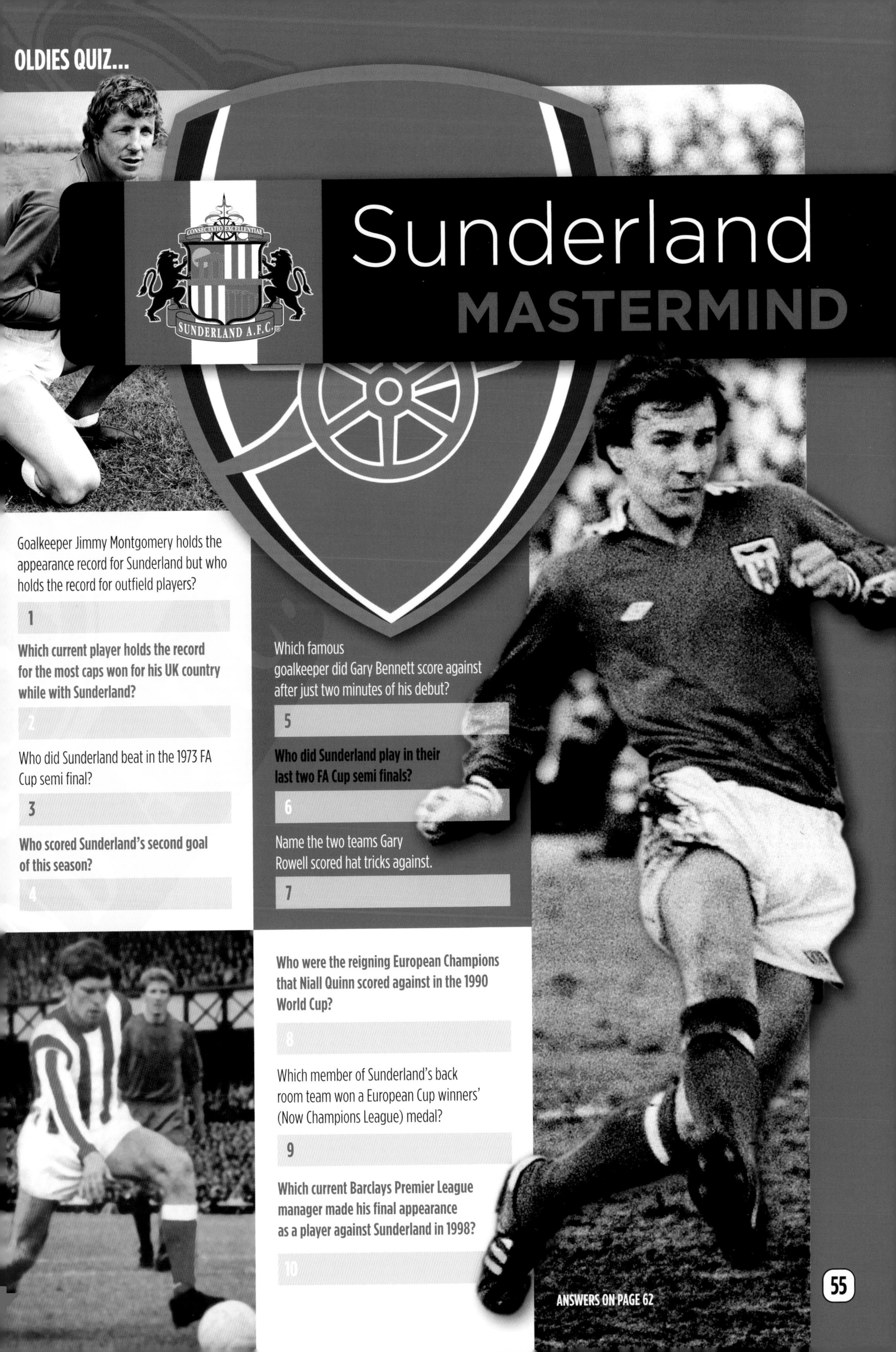

Sunderland MASTERMIND

Goalkeeper Jimmy Montgomery holds the appearance record for Sunderland but who holds the record for outfield players?

1

Which current player holds the record for the most caps won for his UK country while with Sunderland?

2

Who did Sunderland beat in the 1973 FA Cup semi final?

3

Who scored Sunderland's second goal of this season?

4

Which famous goalkeeper did Gary Bennett score against after just two minutes of his debut?

5

Who did Sunderland play in their last two FA Cup semi finals?

6

Name the two teams Gary Rowell scored hat tricks against.

7

Who were the reigning European Champions that Niall Quinn scored against in the 1990 World Cup?

8

Which member of Sunderland's back room team won a European Cup winners' (Now Champions League) medal?

9

Which current Barclays Premier League manager made his final appearance as a player against Sunderland in 1998?

10

ANSWERS ON PAGE 62

Sunderland's ...BIGGEST WINS

BIGGEST EVER LEAGUE WIN

AGAINST: **Newcastle United!!!!**

DATE: December 5th 1908

FACT: This scoreline has never been beaten and is still the record away win by any team in the top flight.

9-1

SATURDAY. DECEMBER 5, 1908.

BIGGEST EVER WIN AT THE STADIUM OF LIGHT

AGAINST: **Oxford Utd**

DATE: September 19th 1998

FACT: Sunderland's best two forwards at this time were Niall Quinn and Kevin Phillips but Phillips wasn't playing and Quinn only came on as sub as he was returning from injury.

7-0

BIGGEST EVER HOME LEAGUE WIN

8-0

AGAINST: Derby County

DATE: September 1st 1894

FACT: It was actually 11-0 overall! The teams kicked without the referee who was late. Sunderland were winning 3-0 when he turned up and made the teams start again at 0-0!

BIGGEST EVER WIN IN THE FA CUP

11-1

AGAINST: Fairfield - a non league team

DATE: February 2nd 1895

FACT: Jimmy Millar became the first of only four players to score five goals in a competitive game for Sunderland. Sunderland also beat non league Chatham Town 9-0 in the FA Cup in 1914.

BIGGEST EVER FA CUP WIN AGAINST A LEAGUE TEAM

7-1

AGAINST: Peterborough United

DATE: February 18th 1967

FACT: All of Sunderland's goals were scored by Scottish players.

BIGGEST EVER HOME LEAGUE CUP WIN

7-0

AGAINST: Oldham Athletic

DATE: September 24th 1962

FACT: Brian Clough scored twice in this match. Ask an old supporter who he was.

BIGGEST EVER: LEAGUE CUP WIN

AGAINST: Cambridge United (Away)

DATE: October 1st 2002

FACT: Manager Peter Reid was sacked after one more game.

...and worst defeats

BIGGEST EVER DEFEAT 0-8

It's happened three times, all in league games

AGAINST: Sheffield Wednesday
West Ham United
Watford

DATE: December 26th 1911
October 19th 1968
25th September 1982

FACT: In the West Ham game Geoff Hurst scored six goals. Two years earlier he'd scored a hat trick for England in the World Cup final.

BIGGEST EVER FA CUP DEFEAT 2-7

AGAINST: Aston Villa

DATE: January 27th 1934

FACT: Sunderland beat Villa 5-1 at home in the league the following week.

BIGGEST EVER LEAGUE CUP DEFEAT 0-6

AGAINST: Derby County

DATE: October 31st 1990

FACT: Sunderland had won 6-1 away to Bristol City in their previous League Cup game.

HIGHEST SCORING DRAW 5-5

AGAINST: Liverpool
Middlesbrough

DATE: January 19th 1907
October 17th 1936

FACT: Sunderland were 4-1 down against Liverpool at half time and leading 4-3 at half time against 'Boro.

Being a footballer isn't simply about practising your skills...

Superfit
...SUNDERLAND

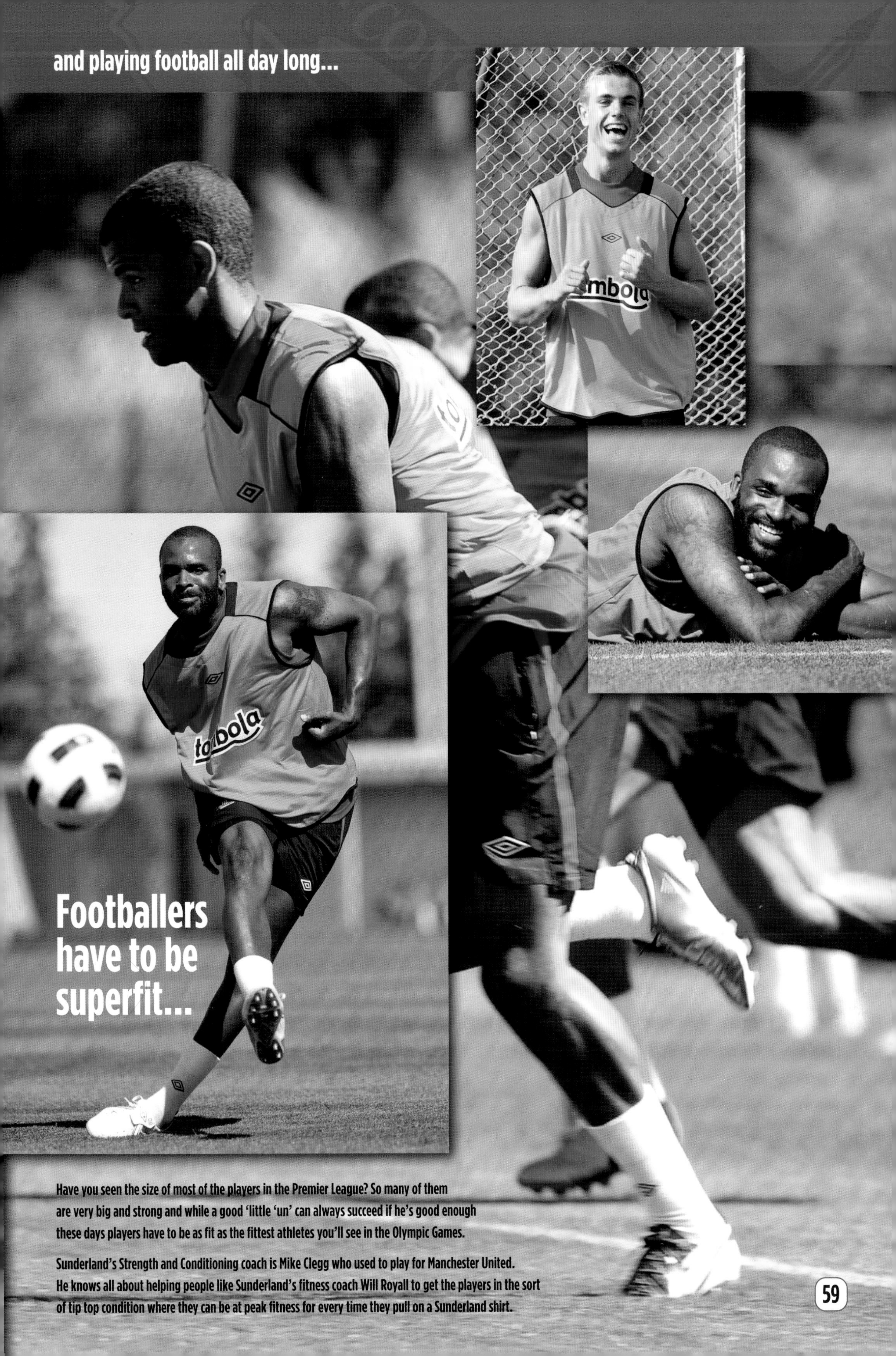

and playing football all day long...

Footballers have to be superfit...

Have you seen the size of most of the players in the Premier League? So many of them are very big and strong and while a good 'little 'un' can always succeed if he's good enough these days players have to be as fit as the fittest athletes you'll see in the Olympic Games.

Sunderland's Strength and Conditioning coach is Mike Clegg who used to play for Manchester United. He knows all about helping people like Sunderland's fitness coach Will Royall to get the players in the sort of tip top condition where they can be at peak fitness for every time they pull on a Sunderland shirt.

Christmas is always an important time in football...

It marks the half way point in the season after which the race for the title, European places, or to secure a place in the following year's Barclays Premier League really hots up. Clubs get money depending upon where they finish in the league so the higher you finish the more money a club receives. Sunderland started this season aiming to get into the top half of the table and better last year's 13th place. However the first half of the campaign has turned out, the remaining months of the season should be exciting.

DECEMBER

Sunday	26	A	Manchester United
Tuesday	**28**	**H**	**Blackpool**

JANUARY

Saturday	**1**	**H**	**Blackburn Rovers**
Wednesday	5	A	Aston Villa
Sunday	**15**	**H**	**Newcastle Utd**
Saturday	22	A	Blackpool

FEBRUARY

Tuesday	**1**	**H**	**Chelsea**
Saturday	5	A	Stoke City
Saturday	**12**	**H**	**Tottenham Hotspur**
Saturday	26	A	Everton

MARCH

Saturday	5	A	Arsenal
Saturday	**19**	**H**	**Liverpool**

APRIL

Saturday	2	A	Manchester City
Saturday	**9**	**H**	**West Bromwich Albion**
Saturday	16	A	Birmingham City
Saturday	**23**	**H**	**Wigan Athletic**
Saturday	**30**	**H**	**Fulham**

MAY

Saturday	7	A	Bolton Wanderers
Saturday	**14**	**H**	**Wolves**
Sunday	22	A	West Ham United

Second half ...OF THE SEASON

What a start it is to the fixture list after Christmas with a trip to Manchester United's Old Trafford on Boxing Day.

That will be a hard game of course but don't forget that last season the Lads produced one of their best performances of the year at Manchester United. Sunderland earned a point from a 2-2 draw that was so nearly what would have been a 2-1 win only for Anton Ferdinand to deflect in an unlucky own goal. You tend to get a lot of games around the Christmas holiday period so it is just two days later that the Stadium of Light will welcome Blackpool.

Blackpool have never played at the Stadium of Light before and are experiencing their first season in the Premier League after a dramatic Play Off final success. Although they haven't been in the top flight for 43 years they were once one of the country's most famous teams. When England won the World Cup in 1966 two members of the squad - Alan Ball and Jimmy Armfield - were Blackpool players and 20 years before Sunderland sensationally won the FA Cup in 1973 Blackpool played in an equally famous final that became known as 'The Matthews Final' after they beat Bolton 4-3. There will be a big holiday crowd at the game that day so make sure you are a part of it!

The first game of 2011 sees Sunderland welcome Blackburn Rovers to the Stadium of Light on New Year's Day before a mid week trip to Aston Villa and then the third round of the FA Cup on the weekend of Saturday January 8th in a week which will also see the beginning of the Carling Cup semi finals.

The game every Sunderland supporter will have been waiting for kicks off at twelve o'clock on Sunday January 16th. That is when local rivals Newcastle United are due at the Stadium of Light. They were beaten 2-1 on their last visit when Sunderland also hit the post and if Sunderland can win again it will be one of the highlights of the season for the red and white army.

The Black Cats play the reverse fixture with Blackpool the following weekend with reigning champions Chelsea being the next game, the Blues being due at the Stadium of Light on Tuesday February 1st just as the transfer window closes a few days after the FA Cup fourth round. Should Sunderland make progress in the FA Cup the 5th round is on February 19th, quarter final on March 12th, semi final on April 16th and the final on May 14th. The Carling Cup final is on Sunday February 27th.

11 days after Chelsea are on Wearside another big London club are due to visit in the shape of Spurs, an away game at Stoke being fitted in between their visits. This comes in the middle of a run of tough fixtures as away games at Everton, Arsenal and Manchester City follow with only a home game against Liverpool in between.

The run in to the end of the season sees Sunderland finish with seven games against teams who finished outside the top eight last season. Home games with newly promoted West Brom, Steve Bruce's old club Wigan, last season's Europa League finalists Fulham and Wolves who are managed by ex Sunderland boss Mick McCarthy are the final four home fixtures.

Away from home Sunderland's last three trips take them to Birmingham, Bolton and West Ham, the final game at West Ham following the home game with Wolves.

As each week ticks by as the end of the season draws near the league gets more and more exciting. Hopefully Sunderland will have good reasons to look back on the 2010-11 campaign once the last ball has been kicked.

ANSWERS

SPOT THE DIFFERENCE · PAGE 26

IDENTITY CRISIS · PAGE 27

MEGA PIXELS
Jordan Henderson

STARS IN THEIR EYES
A. Craig Gordon
B. Andy Reid
C. Michael Turner
D. Darren Bent

TAKE 2
A. Lee Cattermole and Steed Malbranque
B. Kieran Richardson and Fraizer Campbell

SUNDERLAND MASTERMIND

YOUR ANSWERS · PAGE 54
1. Darren Bent. 2. 25. 3. Manchester United.
4. Craig Gordon. 5. Steed Malbranque. 6. Paulo Da Silva, Cristian Riveros, John Mensah and Asamoah Gyan.
7. Da Silva and Riveros played for Paraguay and Mensah and Gyan for Ghana. 8. Elmohamady.
9. Kieran Richardson. 10. Jordan Henderson

ADULTS ANSWERS · PAGE 55
1. Len Ashurst. 2. Craig Gordon for Scotland. 3. Arsenal.
4. It was an own goal by Stephen Carr of Birmingham City.
5. Peter Shilton (now England's record appearance maker).
6. Millwall in 2004 and Norwich City in 1992.
7. Newcastle and Arsenal. 8. Netherlands. 9. Goalkeeping coach Nigel Spink. 10. Steve Bruce (for Sheffield United).